Watch

Go Truck!

By Czeena Devera

② The truck carries dirt.

The truck carries bricks.

4 The truck carries rocks.

The truck carries wood.

The truck carries cement.

The truck carries pipes.

The truck carries tools.

The truck carries machines.

The truck carries trash.

The truck carries cars.

The truck carries boxes.

The truck carries bananas.

Word List

truck	cement	cars
dirt	pipes	boxes
bricks	tools	bananas
rocks	machines	
wood	trash	

The truck carries dirt.

The truck carries bricks.

The truck carries rocks.

The truck carries wood.

The truck carries cement.

The truck carries pipes.

The truck carries tools.

The truck carries machines.

The truck carries trash.

The truck carries cars.

The truck carries boxes.

The truck carries bananas.

Published in the United States of America by Cherry Lake Publishing
Ann Arbor, Michigan
www.cherrylakepublishing.com

Photo Credits: © Sanit Fuangnakhon/Shutterstock.com, front cover, back cover, 1, 15; © mihalec/Shutterstock.com, 2; © Aleksandrn/Dreamstime.com, 3; © Sunshine Seeds/iStockphoto, 4; © steve estvanik/Shutterstock.com, 5; © Blanscape/Shutterstock.com, 6; © obilior/iStockphoto, 7; © VanWyckExpress/iStockphoto, 8; © kozmoat98/iStockphoto, 9; © Africa Studio/Shutterstock.com, 10; © Vibrant Image Studio/Shutterstock.com, 11; © nd3000/Shutterstock.com, 12; © Gualberto Becerra/Shutterstock.com, 13

Cherry Blossom Press is an imprint of Cherry Lake Publishing.

Library of Congress Cataloging-in-Publication Data

Names: Devera, Czeena, author.
Title: Go truck! / Czeena Devera.
Description: Ann Arbor, MI : Cherry Lake Publishing, 2019. | Series: Watch it go |
    Includes bibliographical references and index. | Audience: Pre-school, excluding Kindergarten.
Identifiers: LCCN 2018034501| ISBN 9781534139183 (pbk.) | ISBN 9781534140387 (pdf) |
    ISBN 9781534141582 (hosted ebook)
Subjects: LCSH: Trucks–Juvenile literature. | Reading (Preschool)
Classification: LCC TL230.15 .D48 2019 | DDC 629.224–dc23
LC record available at https://lccn.loc.gov/2018034501

Printed in the United States of America
Corporate Graphics

CHERRY BLOSSOM PRESS